This book belongs to:

____

Made in the USA
Coppell, TX
28 April 2021

54653547R00066